Success Struggles?

Don Barnes

Published by Don Barnes, 2024.

Table of Contents

About the Author

Don is the founder and author of Life Works in Threes!™ E-books. He is a lifelong Texan who has traveled extensively while taking a keen interest in human behavior. His curiosity about life and what drives humans led him to the discovery of how life works in threes. He coined this term as the *Tryune Concept*.

Don attended college on an athletic scholarship and then embarked on a 30-year career in the oil and gas industry. Since the year 2000, he has been a consultant for distributors and manufacturers of various industries. Along the way, he worked on his Tryune discovery in hopes of someday sharing his findings with those struggling unnecessarily... in life. What Don surmised from 40+ years of R&D was that people were struggling unnecessarily because they were not aware that "life works in threes." They, for the most part, have been living their lives <u>by chance</u> rather than <u>by choice,</u> he also discovered.

From this, he began focusing on the "mechanics of life" which shows formulas for success with subjects such as *life, health, money, purpose and so forth*. When people are able to grasp the Tryune Concept, they can apply the formulas with topics that interest them and begin eliminating the struggle. This epiphany is what triggered his Tryune venture and is now on the path of sharing with all who desire to improve on their lives.

Don currently resides in Southern California and Texas while overseeing his businesses and investments.

Life Works in Threes™

When I was a kid growing up, no one sat me down and said, "Okay Don, I'm going to show you how life works so that you can navigate your way through adulthood." I graduated from school, got married and went about my way with the "learn as you go" concept. It was kind of like putting together a backyard swing set without a set of instructions. Lots of frustration and do-overs, for sure!

My discovery of the "triune" word and noticing how things come together in threes is really what set me off on researching that maybe "life comes in three" ...sort of a mechanical approach to managing life, if you will. I combed the libraries and bookstores for information on this and found one book on the subject that was written back in 1951. The author's name was John S. Arant.

What Mr. Arant had to say is this "For lack of a better name, I have called this *The Triangle of Triumph* and therefore, consistent with the name, since most of these conclusions are built on the geometric figure of the triangle." He continued "All Life and all lives are seated in, and circumscribed by, the triangle. The Author and Source and Director of all life is Himself triune in character – Father, Son, and Holy Spirit. Man is of triple nature – body, mind, and spirit – and within those three there are many triangles – desires, development, decay; intellect, will, sensibilities. Of this "paced interlude in the midst of eternity" which we call time there is the triangle of Past, Present, and Future. Space – that limitless and measureless element of the physical universe – is best known in terms of Height, Breadth, and Depth. Try building yourself some triangles along the lines of your Will, your Work, your Way – You will find some interesting angles.

So, for the first time, I realized that life is designed in a mechanical way to come in threes. That means you don't have to rely on wishing and hoping things turn out okay. You can actually look at the three parts that a particular thing is made of and then apply them to get what you're wanting. Like a three-ingredient recipe or a combination lock. With a combination lock, you need the three exact numbers to unlock the lock...otherwise you will continue to struggle.

Some 40 years later, I accumulated things that work in threes and that's when I knew I needed to share this with anyone wanting answers. To have success/harmony in your life, just apply the three parts of an area you're working on, and things will fall into place. I also learned that the recipe for success with just about anything is by doing these three things, consistently – THINK positively, SPEAK positively and ACT positively. For example, if I want to be a successful artist. I would think to myself "I can do this because I have the talent." Then I would speak it this way "Yes, I am working on my art degree and plan to do portraits professionally." Finally, I would act on that by taking art classes and continue crafting my skill. Eventually, I will see the positive results/success I'm looking for.

Conversely, if I think positively but speak negatively...it will cancel out. Or if I speak positively but have no positive action going on...nothing will happen.

I looked up "How Life Works" and "The Mechanics of Life" and these are really talking about the biology of how our cells work and other chemistry. TRYUNE WORKS! teaches that life is kind of like building blocks. Pick a topic you may be struggling with. See the three parts that topic consists of and then start applying them...on a consistent basis. That will help you overcome the struggle and get you back in harmony/success with how life works.

For 30+ years I was a golf instructor (by accident). My two kids had some success playing junior golf and so friends and neighbors would ask me to show them and their kids how to play golf successfully. From all of this, I got pretty good at watching golfers on the driving range and could spot right away why they were struggling with hitting bad golf shots. I was able to do that because I knew the three steps to hitting good golf shots. I learned them from studying golf and played for several decades. I "broke the code" for me so to speak.

So now you know that life works in threes. You can live your life *by choice* rather than *by chance* and that my friend... is the key to a fulfilling life.

LIFE WORKS
IN THREES!

My sanctuary on the Pacific coast

Introduction

Success is one of those fascinating concepts that can wear a different outfit for each person it meets. For some, it's the corner office with a view, a title that gleams on a business card, or hitting that ambitious revenue target. It's that feeling of accomplishment when you've climbed the mountain you set out to conquer. But for others, success might be found in the quiet moments—a cozy evening with loved ones, a hobby that brings joy, or simply being content with where life has taken them.

Think about it: your version of success could be someone else's starting line. We all come from different backgrounds, experiences, and dreams, which color our definition of success in unique ways. It's like having a favorite ice cream flavor—some prefer classic vanilla, while others might go wild for something like cherry Garcia. And that's the beauty of it! Success isn't one-size-fits-all; it's a tailor-made suit that you design to fit your aspirations and values.

In the grand tapestry of life, success isn't just about the destination but the journey you take to get there. It's about the lessons learned, the challenges overcome, and the growth experienced along the way. Whether you measure success in medals won, lives touched, or personal milestones achieved, it's a deeply personal and evolving concept. So, embrace what success means to you, knowing that your definition is as unique and valid as anyone else's. After all, the richness of life lies in its diversity, including how we each define and celebrate our own successes.

My discovery of the Tryune Concept

Before we dive into success struggles and how to overcome them, let me share my discovery of the Tryune Concept and how life works in threes. It all began in the summer of 1982.

I grew up with parents who treated everyone with decency and respect. My three older sisters and I were raised in a home that was "middle-class traditional." We lived in modest homes in different small towns, attended school and church on a regular basis and celebrated all the traditional holidays. Eventually we settled during the spring of 1964 in the big city of Houston, Texas. I'll never forget the vastness of the city and hearing sirens from police cars, fire trucks and ambulances on a regular basis. I was excited and scared at the same time.

Once settled in this fast-paced city, I finished my growing-up years with an academic diploma and sweetheart intact. I got a job, bought a car, got married, bought a house and produced two beautiful babies in a span of about 5 years. Talk about having to grow up fast!

Things went from great in my childhood to absolute misery in my young adulthood. I began to struggle with my job because deep down I just hated what I was doing. This problem created a snowball effect because soon after, my weight, my finances, my relationships, my happiness and everything else worth saving was going down the drain. I eventually hit a level of frustration that I had never experienced before and didn't know how to get out of it. My cry for help was for anyone or anything to come to my rescue. I just ran out of solutions for my situation.

This is when my discovery happened.

One night shortly after my meltdown, while sleeping soundly, the word "triune" began to softly pound in my head like a mantra. I woke up a little startled and decided to go look up the word in my favorite dictionary (this was WAY before Google.) The definition said '**triune** (try-une) – 1) a group of three things; united. 2) Being 3 in 1 such as *humans are mental, physical and spiritual.* I scratched my head, got a glass of water and went back to bed.

The next day while driving around town, I began thinking about things that I was taught in my younger years that came in threes. My Boy Scout manual taught that to have **character**, I needed to be *1) physically strong,* 2) *mentally awake and 3) morally straight.* My high school football coach would say emphatically "If you want to be **a good football player**, you have to be *1) mobile 2) agile and 3) hostile*!" My first sales manager shared with me that to be **a successful salesman**, I needed to have *1) sales skills, 2) product knowledge and 3) a good image.*

"Hmm", I thought, "wonder if there are other examples out there of things that work in threes?" So, some 40 years later, I have researched and discovered that many, many things work in threes. What this message was telling me is that to achieve success or balance in any significant area of my life, the three things that area consisted of had to be present, continuously. That's when I had my epiphany. This discovery was telling me the secret to how life <u>really</u> works...in a mechanical way.

Tryune is a play on the word "triune" as an invitation to "try" this concept. Furthermore, we do not say that life <u>only</u> works in threes. Life also works in ones, twos, fours and so on. What has been observed though is that the many things significant to life, just so happen to come and work in threes. That's what is being shared in this book.

Now, you are about to see 40+ years of research and proof that life works in threes. I did not make up any of these topics. I invite you to research them on the internet to validate what is written here. There are some interesting facts that most of us have never realized...until now.

How Life Works in Threes (around 200 examples)

<u>**LIFE**</u>

Humans consist of *body, mind and soul.*

A human's basic needs are *health, income and provisions.*

A human's basic wants are *comfort, gain and approval.*

Our minds are made up of the *conscious, the subconscious and the unconscious.*

Philosophy explains *the id, the ego and superego.*

Atoms consist of *protons, neutrons and electrons.*

Motion is explained by *three basic laws.*

Science falls under three main branches: *natural, social and formal sciences*

Time is *past, present and future…*at the same time.

Electricity consists of *ohms, amperes and voltage.*

Music's basic elements are *duration, pitch and timbre.*

Democracy is a government *of the people, by the people and for the people.*

U.S. branches of government are *the judicial, the executive and the legislative.*

Armed Forces protect us on *land, air and sea.*

Environmentally, we are asked *to reduce, recycle and re-use.*

The news program gives us *the news, sports and conditions.*

Our days consist of *morning, afternoon and evening.*

Three months in each season of the year

Our main meals are known as *breakfast, lunch and dinner.*

A balanced diet consists of *good proteins, carbohydrates and fats.*

Traditional Family consists of *father, mother, and child(ren)*

<u>SCIENCES</u>

Three major branches of natural science – *(physical, earth/space and life sciences)*

Three major branches of modern physics - *(classical, relativistic, quantum)*

Three major branches of biology *(botany, zoology, microbiology)*

Three spatial dimensions: *height* (up/down), *width* (left/right) and *depth* (forwards/backwards)

Three-gauge bosons (photon, gluon, W&Z bosons)

Three types of elementary particles *(leptons, quarks, gauge bosons)*

Three quarks in every proton *(two "up" and one "down")*

Three primary colors of light *(red, green, blue)*

Three color tone properties *(hue, value, chroma)*

Three laws of motion (*Newton's laws*)

Three laws of planetary motion (*Kepler's laws*)

Three layers of the Sun's interior (*core, radiative zone, convective zone*)

Three layers of the Sun's atmosphere (*photosphere, chromosphere, corona*)

Three types of meteorites (*iron, stony iron, stony*)

Three types of galaxy shapes (*elliptical, spiral, irregular*)

Three substances of the universe (*normal matter, 'dark matter', 'dark energy'*)

Three phases of the moon (*new moon, first quarter, full moon*)

Three planetary regions (*temperate, sub-tropical, tropical*)

Three layers of the Earth (*crust, mantle, core*)

Three components of an ecosystem (*producers, consumers, decomposers*)

Three types of rocks (*igneous, sedimentary, metamorphic*)

Three types of fossil fuels (*coal, crude oil, natural gas*)

Three hydrological processes (*evaporation, condensation, precipitation*)

Three basic types of (meteorological) precipitation (*liquid, freezing, frozen*)

Three types of substances *(mono-constituent, multi-constituent, UVCB)*

Three phases of (normal) matter *(solid, liquid, gas)*

Three types of covalent chemical bonds *(single, double and triple bonds)*

Three isotopes of hydrogen *(protium, deuterium, tritium)*

Three atoms in each molecule of water *(two hydrogen atoms and an oxygen atom)*

Three endings to salts *(-ide, -ite, -ate)*

Three requirements for fire *(fuel, oxygen, heat)*

Three nucleotide bases in a genetic codon

Three domains of life *(archaea, bacteria and eukaryotes)*

Three major groups of flowering plants *(monocots, eudicots, magnolids)*

Three major functions that are basic to plant growth and development: *(photosynthesis* [making sugars], *respiration* [metabolizing those sugars], and *transpiration* [water vapor loss]

Three things that the chlorophyll in plants needs for photosynthesis to take place: *(sunlight, carbon dioxide and water)*

Transpiration serves three roles: *(cooling the plant, moving minerals* and *sugars through the plant,* and *maintaining the turgidity pressure* [stiffness] *of the plant's cells)*

Three parts of an insect's body *(head, thorax, abdomen)*

BIOLOGY

Three types of cones in the retina, relating to the three primary colors

Three semi-circular canals in the ear *(lateral, anterior, posterior)*

Three sections in the ear *(outer, middle, inner)*

Three ossicles in the middle ear *(malleus, incus, stapes)*

Three segments to each limb *(proximal, mid, distal)*

Three bones in each arm *(humerus, radius, ulna)*

Three joints in the arm *(shoulder, elbow, wrist)*

Three joints in the leg *(hip, knee, ankle)*

Three joints in the elbow *(humeroulnar, humeroradial, proximal radioulnar)*

Three functional compartments in the knee joint *(the femoropatellar, medial femorotibial* and *lateral femorotibial articulations)*

Three types of fibrous joints *(sutures, gomphoses, syndesmoses)*

Three types of bone in each hand (*carpals, metacarpals, phalanges*)

Three types of bone in each foot (*tarsals, metatarsals, phalanges*)

Three bones (phalanges) in each finger and in each toe (*proximal, intermediate, distal*)

Three layers of skin (*dermis, epidermis, hypodermis*)

Three components of a cell (*cell membrane, nucleus, cytoplasm*)

Three types of blood vessels (*arteries, veins, capillaries*)

Three types of blood cells [*red* (erythrocytes), *white* (leukocytes), *platelets* (thrombocytes)]

Three processes of the intestinal tract (*ingestion, digestion, excretion*)

Three germ layers (*Endoderm, Mesoderm, Ectoderm*)

Three parts of a human tooth (*crown, neck, root*)

Three organs of otolaryngology (*ear, nose, throat*)

Three major body systems (*digestive, circulatory, respiratory*)

Three parts to a neuron: (*soma* [*cell body*], *axon, dendrites*)

Three main parts of the brain (*forebrain, midbrain, hindbrain*)

Three parts of the forebrain *(cerebrum, thalamus, hypothalamus)*

Three parts of the midbrain *(colliculi, tegmentum, cerebral peduncles)*

Three parts of the hindbrain *(cerebellum, pons, medulla)*

Three membranes enclosing the brain *(dura mater, arachnoid, pia mater)*

The brain operates on three levels: *consciously* (for cognitive thought and declarative memory); *subconsciously* (for pre-planned actions and procedural memory); and *unconsciously* (for breathing, heart beating, etc.)

Our conscious mind is fed from three sources: *our senses* (which can be fooled); *our memory* (which is flawed); and *our imagination* (which is inventive)

Three aspects of the human mind *(memory, intellect, will)*

Three parts of the human personality *(id, ego, superego)*

The sum of human capacity consists of three abilities *(thought, word and deed)*

Three times of man *(birth, life, death)*

Three periods of the Gait Cycle *(initial double limb support, single limb support, and terminal double limb support)*

<u>MUSIC</u>

Three types of musical notes *(sharps, flats, naturals)*

Three aspects of a song (*lyrics, melody, rhythm*)

Three types of musical chords (*root, third, fifth*)

MATHEMATICS

Three types of a real number (*positive, negative, zero*)

Three parts to any arithmetic operation: for addition: *augend, addend and sum* - for subtraction: *minuend, subtrahend and difference* - for multiplication: *multiplicand, multiplier and product* - for division: *dividend, divisor and quotient*

Three laws of arithmetic operations (*commutative, associative, distributive*)

Three types of equivalence relation (*reflexivity, symmetry, transitivity*)

Three types of symmetry operations (*translation, rotation, reflection*)

Three geometries (*Euclidean, spherical, hyperbolic*)

The number *3* is the basis of an entire branch of mathematics, called trigonometry (from the Greek *trigonon* "triangle" + *metron* "measure")

Three trigonometric functions (*sine, cosine, tangent*)

Three types of average (*mean, mode, median*)

GRAMMAR

Three logical operators (*AND, OR and NOT*)

Three laws of logic (*identity, noncontradiction, excluded middle*)

Three parts of a logical syllogism (*major premise, minor premise, conclusion*)

Three grammatical parts to a sentence (*subject, verb, complement*)

Three persons in grammar [*1st person* (I/we), *2nd* (you or your), *3rd* (he/she/it/they)]

Three genders in grammar [*masculine* (he/him), *feminine* (she/her), *neuter* (it)]

Three forms of comparison in grammar [*positive, comparative* (more, -er), *superlative* (most, -est)]

Three cases in (English) grammar [*subjective/nominative* (he), *objective/accusative* (him) and *possessive/genitive* (his)]

Three parts of a narrative (*beginning, middle, end*)

Components of an essay (*introduction, body, conclusion*)

Elements of a rhetorical appeal (*ethos, pathos, logos*)

Aspects of a story (*plot, characters, setting*)

<u>RELIGION</u>

The Creator – *omniscient, omnipotent, omnipresent*

Christian God – *Father, Son, Holy Spirit*

Jesus – *The Way, The Truth, The Life*

Ancient Near East- *Qudshu, Astarte, Anat*

Classical Antiquity – Many dieties came in threes

Hinduism – Para Brahman is *Brahma, Visnu, Shiva*

Ancient Celtic Cultures – *many example of triad dieties*

Buddhism – *The three jewels*

Taoism – *The three pure ones*

Islam – *Fear, Hope and Love*

Baha'i - *Intention, Power and Action*

Confucianism – *Benevolence, Wisdom and Courage*

<u>OTHER TRIUNE EXAMPLES</u>

3 Coins in a Fountain

3 Days of the Condor

3 Miles in a League

3 Goals in a Hat Trick

3 Piece Suit

3 Feet in a Yard

3 Books in Lord of the Rings

3 Ring Circus

3 Ships of Christopher Columbus

3 Sheets to the Wind

3 Books in a Trilogy

3 Wheels on a Tricycle

3 Wise Men

3-Legged Race

3 Ring Circus

3-Wheeler

3 Cornered Hat

3 Dimensional

3 Musketeers

3 R's (reading, 'riting, 'rithmatic)

3 Sides of a triangle

3 Races in the Triple Crown (horse racing)

3 Angles in a Triangle

3 Trimesters in a Pregnancy

3 Flavors in Neapolitan Ice Cream

3 Stars in Orion's belt

3 Barleycorns in an Inch

3 Hands on a Clock (with the Seconds Hand)

3 Colors in a Flag

3 Minute Egg

3 Great Pyramids at Giza

3 Holes in a Bowling Ball

3 Colors in a Set of Traffic Lights

3 Minutes in a Boxing Round

3 Teaspoons in a Tablespoon

3 Legs on a Stool

3 Monastic Vows (Obience, Stability, Conversatio Morum)

3 Body Types: Endomorph, Mesomorph, Ectomorph

3 Ring Notebooks

3 Germ layers: Endoderm, Mesoderm, Ectoderm

3 Species of Homo: Homo habilis, Homo erectus, Homo sapiens

3 Basic parts of a camera: Lens, Shutter, Sensor

3 Stages of a Project lifecycle: initiation, planning, execution

The Truth, The Whole Truth and Nothing but the Truth

Life, Liberty and the Pursuit of Happiness

Hear no Evil, See no Evil, Speak no Evil

National motto of France/Haiti: Liberty, Equality, Fraternity

Paper, Rock, Scissors

Ready, Aim, Fire

On Your mark, Get Set, Go

Olympic medals of gold, silver, bronze

Types of joints (ball & socket, hinge, pivot)

Stages of a rocket launch (launch, orbit, re-entry)

Parts of a joke (setup, delivery, punchline)

Primary components of a transistor (emitter, base, collector)

Primary components of an airplane (fuselage, wings, empennage)

Basic components of a computer: CPU, memory, storage

Three phases in the development of technology (*eotechnic* [*mechanical*], *paleotechnic* [*steam-powered*] and *neotechnic* [*electric-powered*]

Communication systems require three components (*transmitter, channel, receiver*)

The list goes on. See if you can find more examples as they are everywhere in our universe. Now that you know that life works in threes (with proof!), we can begin to apply this concept to whatever topics we want.

So, to overcome struggles with success, we need to apply the three areas that success consists of – THINK, SPEAK and ACT POSITIVELY, continuously. Let's get started!

THINK
SUCCESS
SPEAK
ACTION

SUCCESS

When it comes to navigating the labyrinth of life, thinking, speaking, and action form a powerful trio that can unlock countless doors to success. First off, **thinking** sets the stage. It's like the architect's blueprint, where you map out your goals, dreams, and strategies. Clear, focused thinking helps you clarify what you want and how you're going to achieve it. It's about envisioning possibilities, weighing options, and making informed decisions that pave the way forward.

Next up, **speaking** is where your dreams gain a voice. It's not just about the words you utter but the power they carry. Effective communication bridges gaps, builds relationships, and inspires others to join you on your journey. Whether it's pitching an idea, negotiating a deal, or simply expressing gratitude, how you speak can influence outcomes and shape perceptions. Your words have the potential to create connections and move mountains.

Lastly, **action** is the engine that propels you toward your goals. It's where ideas transform into tangible results. Taking consistent, purposeful action turns aspirations into achievements. It's about rolling up your sleeves, diving in, and persevering through challenges. Every step forward, no matter how small, builds momentum and brings you closer to success. Action transforms dreams from mere possibilities into living, breathing realities.

In essence, *thinking, speaking, and action* form a dynamic trifecta that fuels personal growth and achievement. They're not just steps in a process but the pillars upon which success stands. So, think big, speak boldly, and act decisively—because with these keys in hand, you're equipped to unlock the doors to a fulfilling and successful life.

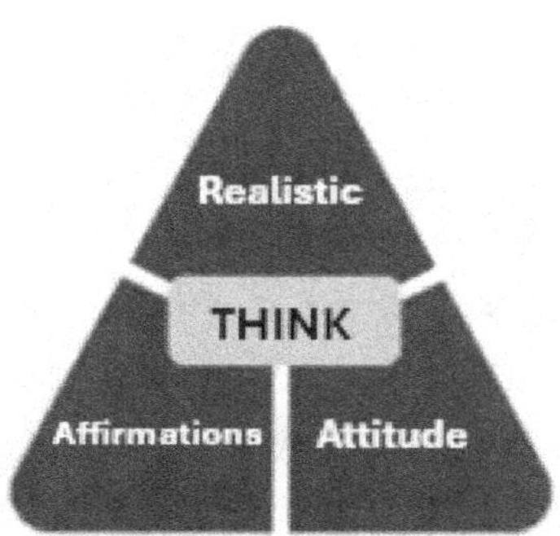
Realistic
THINK
Affirmations
Attitude

THINKING

Positive thinking isn't just about wearing rose-colored glasses—it's a powerful mindset that can shape your reality in remarkable ways. When you cultivate a positive outlook, you're essentially planting seeds of optimism and possibility. This mindset acts like a magnet, drawing opportunities, solutions, and like-minded individuals into your orbit. It's like setting the stage for a vibrant and fulfilling life where challenges become opportunities for growth and setbacks are seen as steppingstones toward success.

Also, positive thinking enhances resilience. It's like having a secret weapon against life's curveballs. Instead of getting bogged down by difficulties, you approach them with a can-do attitude and a belief in your ability to overcome. This resilience not only helps you bounce back stronger but also fosters a mindset of continuous improvement. You start seeing setbacks as temporary detours rather than roadblocks, which fuels your determination to keep moving forward.

Finally, positive thinking fuels motivation and action. When you believe in your goals and envision success, you're more likely to take proactive steps toward achieving them. It's like having a built-in motivational coach cheering you on from the sidelines. Whether it's pursuing a new career path, starting a business venture, or making positive changes in your personal life, your optimistic mindset becomes the driving force behind your actions. And as you take consistent steps toward your dreams, you'll find that positive thinking not only sets the stage but also becomes the catalyst for turning your aspirations into reality.

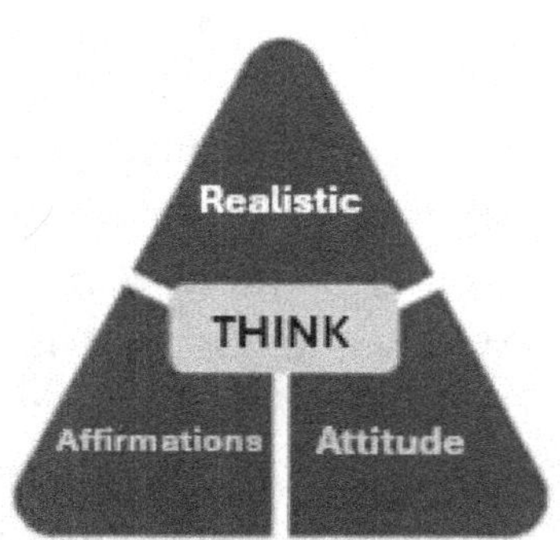

Realistic
THINK
Affirmations
Attitude

Realistic

Setting goals is like charting a course for your dreams, but being realistic about them ensures you're on a path that's both achievable and fulfilling. When you set realistic goals, you're essentially setting yourself up for success. It's about finding that sweet spot between ambition and practicality—challenging yourself while also acknowledging your current resources, capabilities, and limitations. This approach not only boosts your confidence as you achieve milestones but also maintains your motivation for the long haul.

Realistic goal setting helps you stay grounded. It's like having a compass that keeps you oriented toward what's feasible and meaningful. By assessing your strengths and weaknesses realistically, you can tailor your goals to match your current circumstances and timeline. This prevents the frustration of setting overly lofty goals that might lead to burnout or disappointment. Instead, you create a roadmap that's clear, actionable, and adaptable to the twists and turns of life.

Being realistic about goal setting fosters a sense of accountability and commitment. When you set goals that are within your reach, you're more likely to stay dedicated to the journey. Each small victory becomes a steppingstone toward larger achievements, reinforcing your belief in your ability to make progress. It's like building a sturdy foundation for your dreams, brick by brick. So, whether it's personal growth, career aspirations, or health goals, being realistic about goal setting ensures you're not just dreaming but actively working toward a future that's both inspiring and attainable.

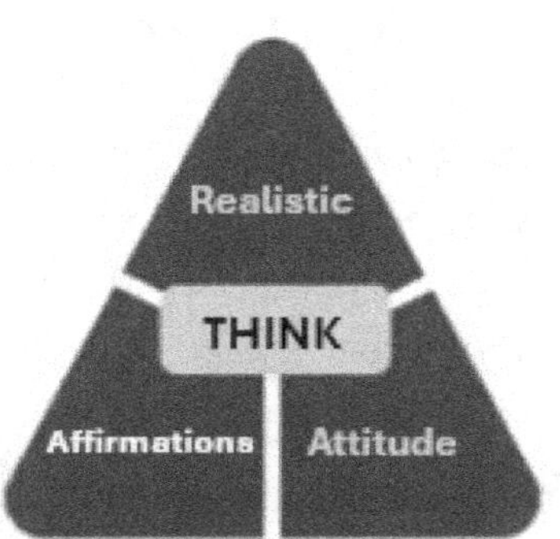
Realistic
THINK
Affirmations
Attitude

Affirmations

Affirmations are like the secret sauce that adds flavor and power to your pursuit of success. They're positive statements you repeat to yourself regularly, aimed at instilling a mindset of confidence, determination, and belief in your abilities. By affirming your goals and qualities, you're essentially programming your mind for success. It's like giving yourself a daily pep talk that reinforces your aspirations and bolsters your resilience in the face of challenges.

Firstly, affirmations help shape your mindset and attitude towards success. When you repeatedly affirm positive statements such as "I am capable," "I am resilient," or "I am worthy of success," you're rewiring your subconscious mind. This creates a mental environment where self-doubt takes a back seat, and self-belief takes the wheel. Affirmations act as a powerful tool to counteract negative self-talk and cultivate a mindset that embraces opportunities and solutions.

Secondly, affirmations enhance focus and motivation. By regularly affirming your goals, whether they're related to career, personal growth, relationships, or health, you keep them at the forefront of your mind. This constant reminder fuels your motivation to take consistent action towards achieving those goals. It's like having a beacon that guides you through distractions and setbacks, reminding you of your purpose and keeping you aligned with your aspirations.

Finally, affirmations contribute to a positive feedback loop of success. When you affirm your goals and visualize your achievements, you're priming yourself to notice and seize opportunities that align with your desires. This proactive mindset not only attracts positive outcomes but also strengthens your belief in your ability to create the life you envision. So, whether you're aiming for career milestones, personal fulfillment, or overall well-being, incorporating affirmations into your daily routine can amplify your efforts and propel you toward success with confidence and clarity.

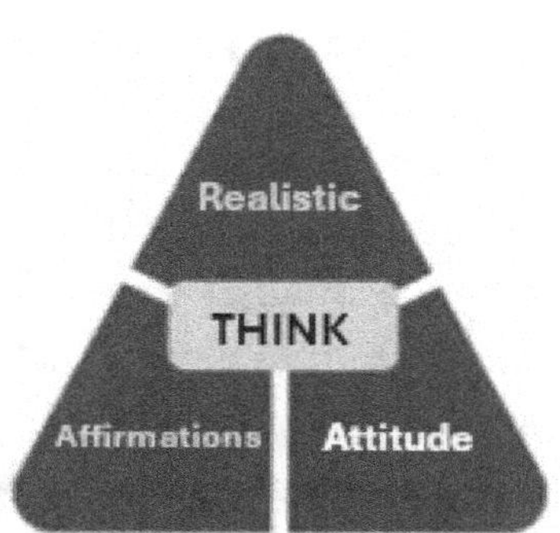

Realistic
THINK
Affirmations
Attitude

Attitude

Maintaining a determined attitude is like having a steadfast companion on your journey to success. It's more than just staying positive—it's about cultivating a mindset that refuses to be swayed by obstacles or setbacks. When you approach your goals with determination, you're essentially committing to pushing forward, no matter the challenges that may arise. This resilience not only strengthens your resolve but also inspires others around you, creating a ripple effect of motivation and perseverance.

A determined attitude fuels perseverance. Success rarely comes without its share of trials and tribulations. It's like navigating a maze where each twist and turn tests your commitment to reaching the goal. With determination as your compass, you're better equipped to weather the storms and stay focused on the prize. It's about embracing the journey, learning from setbacks, and finding creative solutions to overcome obstacles along the way.

Maintaining a determined attitude fosters personal growth and resilience. When faced with adversity, your determination acts as a catalyst for growth. It's like turning challenges into opportunities to hone your skills, expand your capabilities, and discover untapped strengths. This growth mindset not only propels you closer to your goals but also prepares you to handle future challenges with greater confidence and grace. So, whether you're pursuing career ambitions, personal development goals, or dreams yet to be realized, nurturing a determined attitude ensures that you stay steadfast on the path to success, equipped with the grit and resilience needed to turn aspirations into achievements.

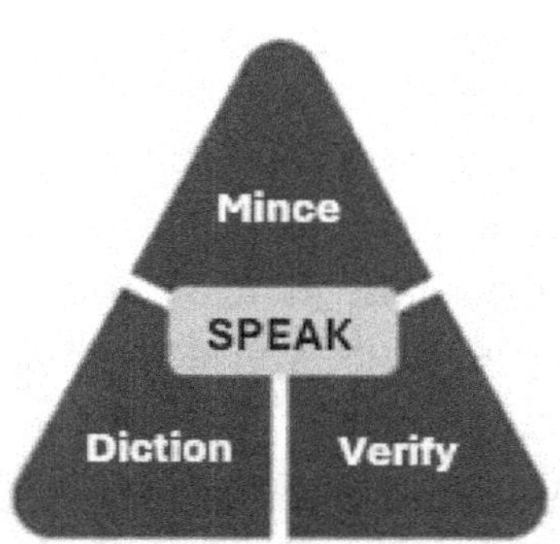
Mince
SPEAK
Diction
Verify

SPEAKING

The words we choose have incredible power—they're like the bridge that connects our thoughts with the outside world. When we take the time to select our words carefully, ensuring they reflect our true thoughts and intentions, we create alignment between our inner and outer selves. This alignment not only enhances clarity in communication but also strengthens our authenticity and credibility. It's like ensuring that the message we send out accurately represents who we are and what we stand for.

Choosing words that are in sync with our thinking fosters better understanding and connection with others. Effective communication isn't just about conveying information—it's about building relationships and creating shared meaning. When our words authentically reflect our thoughts and beliefs, they resonate with others on a deeper level. This authenticity builds trust and rapport, fostering stronger connections and collaborations. It's like speaking a language that everyone can understand and relate to, promoting openness and mutual respect.

Carefully chosen words can inspire and motivate. Whether we're articulating our goals, expressing gratitude, or offering encouragement, the way we phrase our thoughts can have a profound impact on ourselves and those around us. Positive and empowering words have the ability to uplift spirits, ignite passion, and spur action. They create a supportive environment where aspirations flourish and people feel empowered to pursue their dreams. So, by consciously selecting words that align with our thoughts and intentions, we not only enhance our communication but also contribute to a more harmonious and encouraging world where words have the power to shape reality for the better.

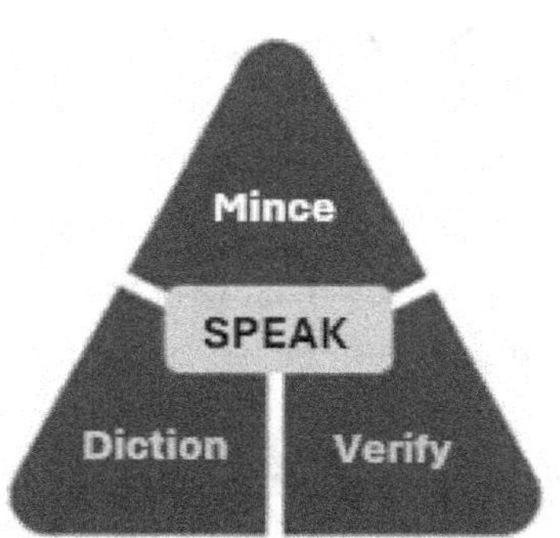
Mince
SPEAK
Diction
Verify

Mince

There's a wonderful saying that goes, "We have two ears and one mouth for a reason"—and it speaks volumes about the importance of listening more than we speak. Mincing our words, or choosing them thoughtfully, is not just about how we express ourselves but also about how we engage with others. When we listen attentively before speaking, we show respect and empathy, fostering deeper connections and understanding in our interactions. It's like creating a space where everyone's voice is heard and valued.

Mincing words encourages effective communication. By carefully choosing what we say and how we say it, we can convey our thoughts and emotions more clearly and diplomatically. This reduces misunderstandings and promotes constructive dialogue, whether we're discussing ideas, resolving conflicts, or offering feedback. It's about using our words intentionally to build bridges of mutual respect and cooperation, rather than unintentionally causing rifts or hurt feelings.

Also, mincing words cultivates mindfulness and self-awareness. When we pause to consider our words before speaking, we become more attuned to the impact they may have on others. This mindful approach not only enhances our communication skills but also encourages personal growth. It's like exercising a muscle of empathy and sensitivity, which strengthens our relationships and contributes to a more harmonious social environment. So, by embracing the wisdom of listening twice as much as we speak and choosing our words with care, we create spaces where understanding flourishes, connections deepen, and positivity thrives.

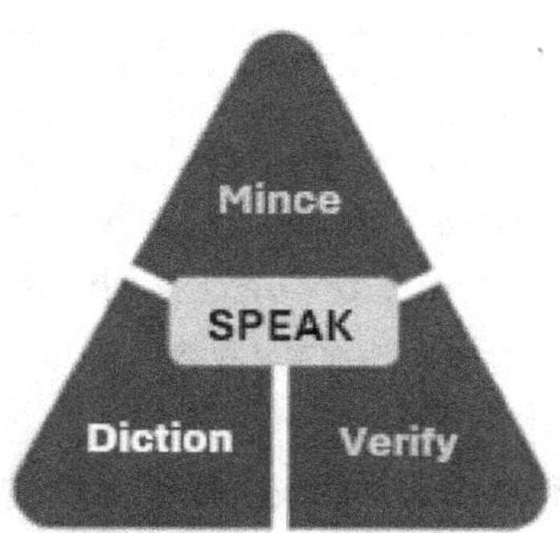
Mince
SPEAK
Diction
Verify

Diction

Proper diction plays a crucial role in effective communication, enhancing clarity, understanding, and respect in our interactions with others. When we pay attention to our diction—how we pronounce words, articulate sentences, and convey meaning—we ensure that our message is delivered accurately and comprehensibly. It's like polishing a gemstone to reveal its true brilliance, ensuring that our words shine brightly and resonate with those we communicate with.

Proper diction reflects professionalism and confidence. Whether in professional settings, social gatherings, or everyday conversations, clear and articulate speech commands attention and conveys competence. It's like dressing for success verbally presenting ourselves with eloquence and precision. This not only boosts our credibility but also fosters trust and respect from those around us. When our words are well-chosen and clearly enunciated, they demonstrate respect for our listeners and affirm our commitment to effective communication.

Suffice it to say, proper diction promotes inclusivity and understanding. In diverse communities and multicultural settings, clear pronunciation and thoughtful phrasing help bridge language barriers and ensure everyone can participate meaningfully in conversations. It's like speaking a universal language of respect and consideration, where everyone feels heard and valued. By refining our diction, we create an environment where communication flows smoothly, ideas are exchanged freely, and relationships are strengthened. So, whether we're addressing a crowd, conversing one-on-one, or participating in group discussions, the importance of proper diction cannot be overstated—it's the key to fostering meaningful connections and building a foundation of mutual understanding and respect.

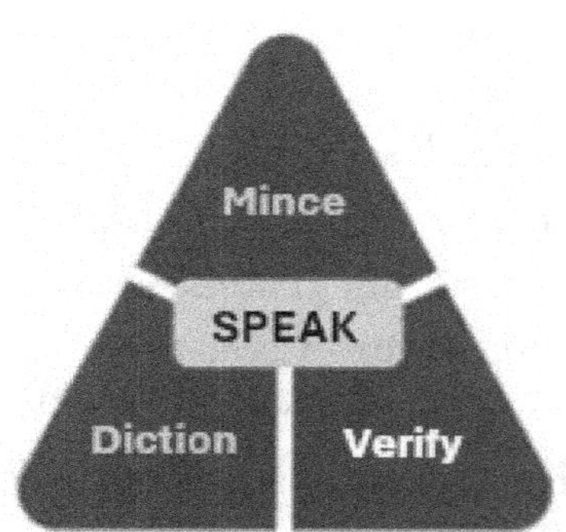
Mince
SPEAK
Diction
Verify

Verify

Verifying information before sharing it with others is not just about accuracy—it's about being a responsible and trustworthy communicator. In today's fast-paced world where information spreads quickly, taking the time to confirm facts ensures that we contribute to informed discussions and avoid spreading misinformation or rumors. It's like being a reliable source in a sea of noise, where our words carry weight and credibility.

Also, verifying information demonstrates respect for the truth and for those we engage with in conversation. When we take the initiative to verify facts before speaking, we show integrity and sincerity in our communication. This builds trust and confidence in our relationships, whether with colleagues, friends, or acquaintances. It's like laying a foundation of honesty and reliability, where our words reflect our commitment to accuracy and thoughtful discourse.

Finally, verifying information helps us make informed decisions and contribute meaningfully to discussions. By ensuring the validity of our sources and the accuracy of our statements, we enhance the quality of our contributions. It's like sharpening a tool before using it, ensuring that our insights and perspectives are grounded and add value to the conversation. Whether discussing current events, sharing knowledge, or offering opinions, the practice of verifying information before speaking is essential for fostering constructive dialogue and promoting mutual understanding. So, by embracing a habit of fact-checking and confirming details, we not only uphold our own credibility but also contribute positively to a culture of responsible communication and informed discourse.

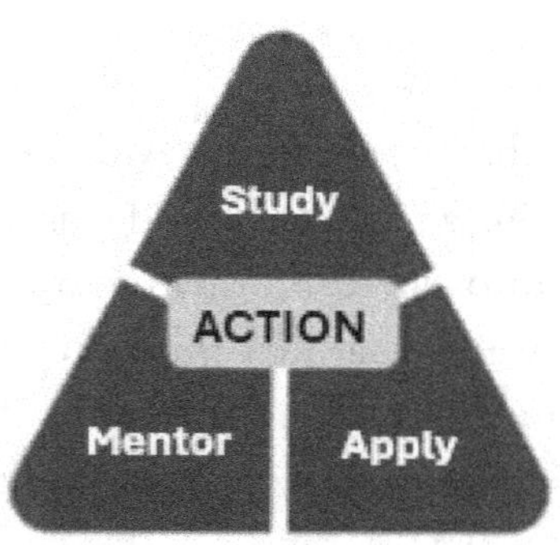
Study
ACTION
Mentor
Apply

ACTION

Let's say that the thing you want to be successful at is getting a promotion at work so you can make more pay. How do you go about doing that? Here's three action steps to get there:

Study – the foundation for any job is to understand the nomenclature or lingo of a business. This is a continuous action because there are always new things to learn. You can study books, take a class, watch videos, read trade magazines and study the company manual. Committing yourself to studying on a continuous basis will give you the credibility needed to take the position ahead of you. Other managers will see that you have a solid foundation for the business and can step into that role if they need you.

Mentor – finding a mentor to work with you is a huge advantage because he/she can share some things with you that are not in a book. This action will save your months and years of learning "the hard way." When you have a mentor that will share his/her experiences, this will save many headaches and remind you of what's coming in the future. Finding a mentor can be done at your workplace or industry association. Through networking, you will meet the pros in the business and hopefully catch someone's attention to help you.

Apply – as you're learning and getting advice, you can also start applying what you've learned. Study the habits of your bosses and emulate them. If they come in at 6:00 or 7:00 a.m., do the same even if you are only required to be at work by 8:00 a.m. Remember, while most employees work eight-hour days, managers usually work 10–12-hour days. Pick the brains of your superiors and ask if there is anything you can help them with. This will show that you are up to the task of whatever it is they are doing. Making points with your superiors is a good way to get promoted.

Assuming the role of the position you're interested in is a good way to show your superiors that you are already up to the task. When the time comes, it will be easy for them to recommend you because you have already shown them that you can do what needs to be done.

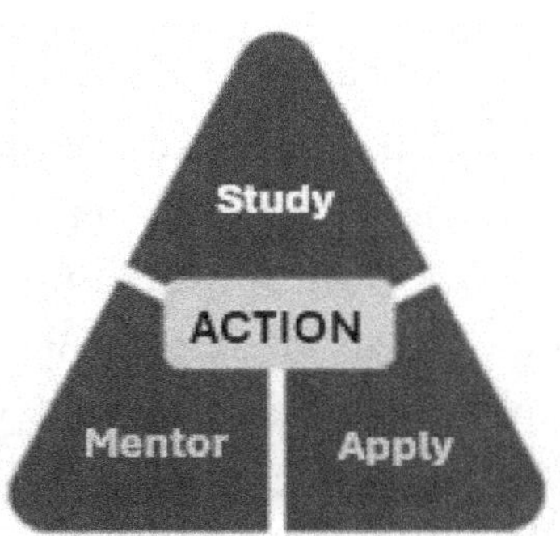
Study
ACTION
Mentor
Apply

Study

Studying isn't just about hitting the books during school years—it's a lifelong journey of discovery, growth, and personal enrichment. Embracing the idea that learning continues throughout our lives opens endless opportunities for personal development and fulfillment. It's like having a passport to explore new ideas, skills, and perspectives that enrich our understanding of the world and ourselves.

Lifelong learning keeps our minds agile and adaptable. In a rapidly changing world where new technologies, ideas, and challenges emerge constantly, staying curious and open to learning ensures that we remain relevant and resilient. It's like staying ahead of the curve, continuously upgrading our mental toolkit with the latest knowledge and skills. This ongoing process of intellectual engagement not only enhances our problem-solving abilities but also fosters creativity and innovation in all aspects of life.

Studying as a lifelong process encourages personal growth and fulfillment. Whether we're exploring a new hobby, mastering a language, or diving into a subject we've always been curious about, each learning endeavor expands our horizons and enriches our experiences. It's like nourishing our minds and spirits with new insights and discoveries that bring joy and satisfaction. By embracing studying as a lifelong commitment, we cultivate a mindset of growth and possibility, continuously evolving into the best versions of ourselves. So, whether you're embarking on a formal course of study or pursuing knowledge independently, remember that the journey of learning is infinite and endlessly rewarding—a lifelong adventure waiting to unfold.

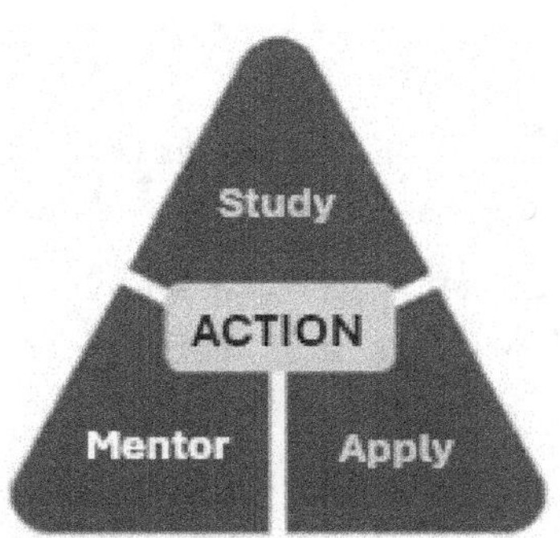
Study
ACTION
Mentor
Apply

Mentor

Having a mentor can be a game-changer as you navigate the path toward success in your endeavors. A mentor is like a trusted guide, someone who has walked the road you aspire to travel and can offer valuable insights, advice, and support based on their own experiences. They provide a unique perspective and wisdom that can help you avoid pitfalls, overcome challenges, and seize opportunities that you might not have recognized on your own. It's like having a seasoned navigator by your side, steering you toward your goals with clarity and confidence.

Mentors offer personalized guidance and encouragement. They take the time to understand your strengths, weaknesses, and aspirations, tailoring their advice to your specific needs and circumstances. This personalized approach not only accelerates your learning and growth but also boosts your self-confidence and resilience. It's like having a cheerleader in your corner, cheering you on through setbacks and celebrating your victories, big and small.

Finally, mentors foster professional and personal development. Beyond practical advice, they can provide constructive feedback, challenge your assumptions, and help you expand your skills and capabilities. Their mentorship can open doors to new opportunities, expand your network, and introduce you to valuable connections within your industry or field of interest. It's like having a door-opener who believes in your potential and is invested in your success. By cultivating a mentorship relationship, you not only gain from their knowledge and experience but also contribute to a supportive community where learning and growth thrive. So, whether you're embarking on a new career path, launching a business, or pursuing personal goals, having a mentor can be a transformative partnership that propels you toward success with guidance, wisdom, and unwavering support.

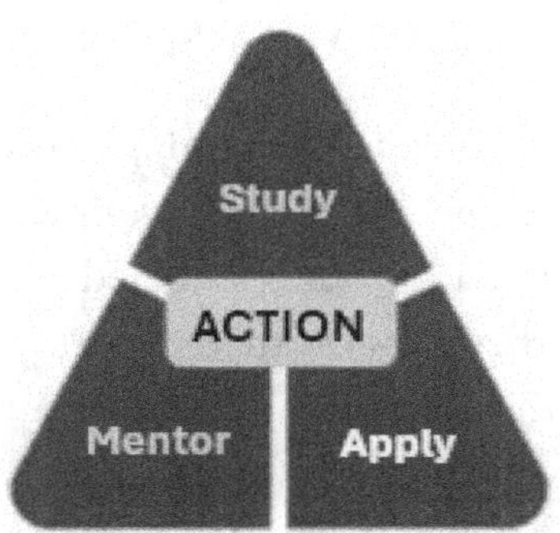
Study
ACTION
Mentor
Apply

Apply

Applying what you've learned is like turning knowledge into action—an essential step toward achieving success in your endeavors. Mentors offer valuable insights, advice, and strategies based on their experiences, but it's through applying these lessons that you truly harness their wisdom and make meaningful progress. It's like having a toolbox filled with the best tools; using them effectively is what gets the job done.

Also, applying what you've studied, and your mentor's teachings demonstrates initiative and commitment. It shows that you value this guidance and are dedicated to integrating their wisdom into your journey. This proactive approach not only accelerates your growth but also strengthens your relationship with your mentor. It's like showing gratitude for their investment in your development by actively striving to improve and succeed.

Finally, applying what you've learned from study and your mentors fosters continuous improvement and innovation. By experimenting with new strategies, refining your skills, and adapting to changing circumstances, you cultivate a mindset of growth and resilience. This iterative process of learning from experience, adjusting course, and persevering through challenges is crucial for long-term success. It's like honing your craft through practice and iteration, steadily advancing toward your goals with confidence and adaptability.

So, whether you're refining your leadership style, implementing new business tactics, or navigating personal growth opportunities, applying the insights gleaned from your mentors transforms knowledge into capability and propels you forward on your path to success.

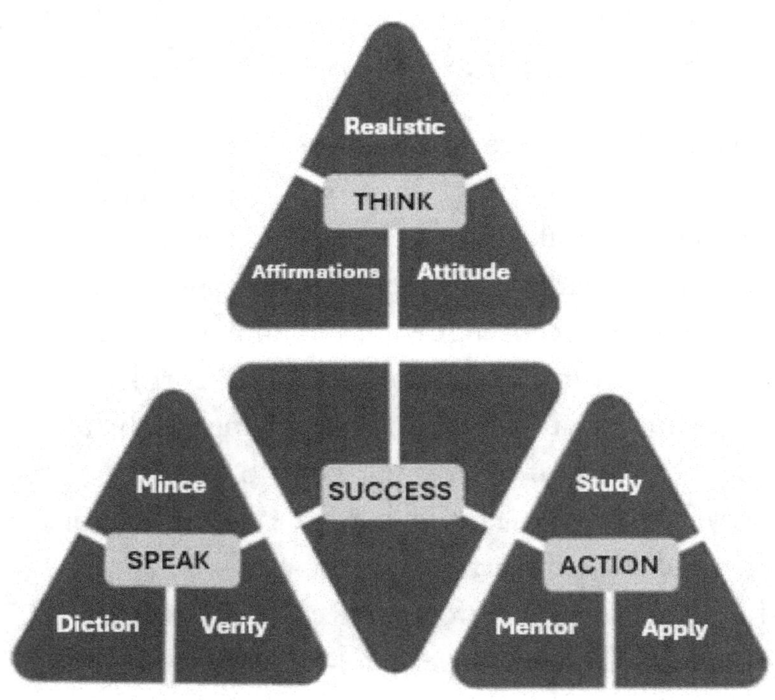

Realistic
THINK
Affirmations
Attitude
Mince
SUCCESS
Study
SPEAK
ACTION
Diction
Verify
Mentor
Apply

BONUS CHAPTER – LIFE IS LIVED OUTSIDE OF OUR COMFORT ZONE

Living outside of our comfort zone is where true growth and fulfillment often occur. When we step beyond familiar boundaries, we challenge ourselves to learn, adapt, and evolve. This journey is marked by experiences that push us to discover our capabilities and strengths. In unfamiliar territory, we are forced to confront uncertainties and take risks, fostering resilience and creativity in problem-solving. Each step taken outside our comfort zone contributes to personal development, as we learn to navigate new situations with courage and adaptability.

Life outside our comfort zone encourages us to embrace change and welcome new perspectives. It cultivates a mindset of openness and curiosity, enabling us to explore diverse opportunities and possibilities. By stretching beyond what is known and comfortable, we expand our horizons and cultivate a deeper understanding of ourselves and the world around us. This process fosters personal growth, enriches our experiences, and broadens our sense of empathy and compassion for others.

Finally, living outside our comfort zone often leads to achieving goals and aspirations that once seemed out of reach. It requires perseverance and determination, as we push through setbacks and challenges. The accomplishments made in unfamiliar territory bring a profound sense of satisfaction and fulfillment, reinforcing our belief in our abilities and potential. Ultimately, life lived outside our comfort zone is dynamic and transformative, offering opportunities for self-discovery, personal growth, and meaningful connections with others. It encourages us to embrace uncertainty and embrace the journey of continuous learning and self-improvement.

SUMMARY

As stated earlier, success isn't one-size-fits-all—it's about living life on your own terms and finding fulfillment in the journey you carve out for yourself. When you define success based on your values, passions, and aspirations, you embrace authenticity and personal satisfaction. It's like crafting a unique masterpiece that reflects who you are and what truly matters to you.

Living life in your own way empowers you to pursue happiness and meaning according to your own compass. It's about embracing your individuality and making choices that resonate with your innermost desires, rather than conforming to external expectations or societal norms. This path to success isn't about comparing yourself to others or chasing someone else's definition of achievement—it's about honoring your dreams and embracing the freedom to chart your own course.

Finally, living authentically leads to a deeper sense of fulfillment and purpose. When you align your actions with your values and follow your passions, you cultivate a life rich in meaning and contentment. It's like finding your own North Star and navigating by its light, confidently embracing opportunities and challenges along the way. This journey of self-discovery and self-expression not only enriches your personal growth but also inspires others to embrace their unique paths to success. So, whether you're pursuing career goals, nurturing relationships, or exploring new adventures, remember that true success lies in living authentically and wholeheartedly making your own choices and shaping your own story with joy, resilience, and purpose.

Invitation

"Knowledge is nice but what we're after is wisdom."

To be successful at something requires a 3-step process of *study, mentoring* and *experience*. I'm going to use the analogy of an auto mechanic to explain what I mean.

Let's say that I desire to be an auto mechanic. Here are the steps to take in order to have success doing that. The first thing will be to take a class or go online and study the terminology of auto mechanics. Studying will be a forever thing because there is so much to learn and things change over time...with new technology coming along.

The second step in this 3-part process is to find a mentor to watch over me and share any insights that he/she might have that aren't in books. A mentor is someone with years of experience and is interested in passing along any wisdom he/she has accumulated over time. This is also a forever thing.

Finally, it's time for experience. That's when we open the hood of automobiles and get familiar with auto parts and their function in running a car/truck. It will be clumsy at first but over time and repetition, it will become second-nature.

So, there you have it. Study, mentoring and experience is the recipe for success in being an auto mechanic or anything else that you desire. You see, knowledge, in and of itself is just information. Advice from a mentor, in and of itself is just trade secrets. And of course, experience is just that... experience. But when you combine all three, then you have wisdom and that is what brings you success.

1. **Study** – to get the lingo down
2. **Mentor** – for trade secrets
3. **Experience** – to actually know what you're doing

This is the formula for success.

When you're with someone who is sharing their struggles with you...just smile at him/her and give them one of these. He/she will ask "What is that?" Then simply reply "Life Works in Threes."

Other titles coming out:

- ◇ **Weight Struggles?**
- ◇ **Abundance Struggles?**
- ◇ **Parenting Struggles?**
- ◇ **Life Struggles?**
- ◇ **Purpose Struggles?**
- ◇ **Happiness Struggles?**
- ◇ **Sales Struggles?**
- ◇ **Speaker Struggles?**
- ◇ **Time Struggles?**
- ◇ **Network Struggles?**
- ◇ **Marriage Struggles?**
- ◇ **Divorce Struggles?**
- ◇ **Money Struggles?**
- ◇ **Career Struggles?**
- ◇ **Dating Struggles?**
- ◇ **Caretaker Struggles?**
- ◇ **Forgiveness Struggles?**
- ◇ **Grieving Struggles?**
- ◇ **Romance Struggles?**
- ◇ **Golf Struggles?**
- ◇ **Workplace Struggles?**
- ◇ **Stress Struggles?**
- ◇ **Shame/Guilt Struggles?**
- ◇ **Addiction Struggles?**

Quotes about Success

"Success is stumbling from failure to failure with no loss of enthusiasm." - Winston S. Churchill

"Success is liking yourself, liking what you do, and liking how you do it." - Maya Angelou

"Only you can determine what success is for you. That's really all that matters."

- Don Barnes

"Success is about challenging yourself to be the best you can be at whatever interests you." - Unknown

"Success breeds confidence and confidence breeds success." - Kenny Rogers

There are several reasons why some people may struggle with achieving success in life:

1. **Fear of Failure**: Some individuals are afraid to take risks or step out of their comfort zone due to the fear of failing. This fear can paralyze them from pursuing opportunities that could lead to success.
2. **Lack of Self-Confidence**: A lack of belief in oneself can prevent individuals from setting ambitious goals or persisting in the face of setbacks. Low self-confidence can also hinder their ability to network effectively or seize opportunities.
3. **Procrastination**: Putting off important tasks or decisions can delay progress towards achieving goals. Chronic procrastination can lead to missed opportunities and a sense of being stuck.
4. **Negative Mindset**: Pessimism, self-doubt, and a generally negative outlook can sabotage efforts to achieve success. A negative mindset can manifest as self-sabotage or reluctance to take necessary actions.
5. **Lack of Clear Goals**: Without clear, specific goals, individuals may lack direction and a sense of purpose. This can lead to drifting through life without making meaningful progress towards success.
6. **Poor Time Management**: Ineffective time management can result in missed deadlines, unfinished projects, and a general sense of being overwhelmed. This can derail efforts to achieve success.
7. **Lack of Resilience**: Inability to bounce back from failures or setbacks can prevent individuals from

learning and growing. Resilience is crucial for navigating challenges on the path to success.

8. **Underestimating the Importance of Skills Development**: Success often requires continuous learning and skill development. Individuals who do not invest in developing relevant skills may find it difficult to compete in their field or adapt to changes.

9. **Unsupportive Environment**: A lack of encouragement or support from family, friends, or peers can make it challenging for individuals to pursue their goals with confidence. Negative influences can undermine motivation and determination.

10. **Fear of Success**: Surprisingly, some individuals may fear the responsibilities, attention, or changes that come with success. This fear can unconsciously lead them to sabotage their own efforts or avoid opportunities for advancement.

These factors can interact in complex ways, making it difficult for some individuals to achieve their full potential and experience success in various aspects of life.

The real definition
of success is -

Living your life

in your own way.

Always striving but never arriving dilemma

The dilemma of always striving but never arriving encapsulates a persistent challenge faced by many individuals on their journey towards success and fulfillment. It often manifests as a continuous pursuit of goals, ambitions, or ideals that seem perpetually out of reach. This paradox can evoke feelings of frustration, disillusionment, or a sense of being stuck in an endless cycle of effort without tangible rewards.

At its core, this dilemma reflects the complexity of personal growth and achievement. It highlights the tension between ambition and contentment, where the desire for progress clashes with the need for present-moment satisfaction. Those who experience this dilemma may find themselves constantly setting new goals or benchmarks, driven by an insatiable thirst for improvement or validation. Yet, despite their efforts and achievements, they may still feel a sense of incompleteness or dissatisfaction.

Moreover, this dilemma can stem from external pressures or societal expectations that perpetuate a culture of perpetual striving. The emphasis on success as an endpoint rather than a continuous journey can create unrealistic standards and foster a mentality of "never enough." As a result, individuals may overlook their current accomplishments or fail to appreciate the progress they have made, constantly chasing the next milestone or benchmark.

However, navigating this dilemma also offers opportunities for introspection and growth. It encourages individuals to reevaluate their motivations and redefine their definitions of success and fulfillment. By embracing a mindset of gratitude and acknowledging their achievements along the way, individuals can find a balance between ambition and contentment. This process requires patience, self-awareness, and a willingness to cultivate resilience in the face of setbacks.

Ultimately, the dilemma of always striving but never arriving underscores the importance of finding joy and meaning in the journey itself. It invites individuals to embrace the present moment, celebrate their accomplishments, and recognize that true fulfillment often lies not in reaching a destination, but in the continuous process of growth, learning, and self-discovery.

It's great to be successful, let's just make sure it's done in a healthy way.

When someone is struggling with a particular area or two, chances are they are "out of balance" with how life works. How does life work? Life works in threes.

If you're interested in personal topics like life, health, money or business topics like sales, time management and public speaking...Life Works in Threes! can shed some light on creating success in those areas.

The definition of TRIUNE is a group of three things; united. Being three in one, such as - humans are *mental, physical* and *spiritual beings*. The word TRYUNE is a play of the word TRIUNE, encouraging all to try this concept and help eliminate struggling unnecessarily.

LifeWorksInThrees.com

9 798227 156723